Server Training Manual

By D. Lee Lott

Text Copyright 2012

All Rights Reserved

Table of Contents

Welcome! 4

    Front of the House Team 5

    Opening Side Work 6

    Know Your Menu 7

    Answering the Phone 9

    Service Sequence 10

    Alcohol Service 12

    Taking and Delivering Orders 13

    Entering orders 18

    Handling Complaints 19

    Check Presentation 21

    Reset Tables 22

    Leaving Early 23

    Tips 24

    General Safety 25

    Closing Side Work 26

Welcome!

You were selected to join our team because you displayed the qualities we look for in an employee that will help us to be successful.

You are an important part of our success!

Our main focus is on teamwork and giving every guest that enters our restaurant a good dining experience.

You are one of the team members that we are depending on to do that.

Front of the House Team

We all work together as a team to create a well-oiled machine that serves our guests. The Front of the House team consists of the Front of the House Manager, Servers, hosts/hostesses, bartenders and busers. Get to know your team members and learn how to work well with them. They will provide you with the backup you may need to give guests the excellent dining experience that we want each of them to have.

Opening Side Work

Shift prep work is to be completed by _____ a.m. for the morning shift and _____ p.m. for the evening shift.

Check that tables and chairs are aligned to the floor plan.

Check silverware, making sure there is enough to get through a busy shift. When rolling silverware, make sure the pieces match and are in good condition (give damaged silverware to the manager). Silverware should ALWAYS be picked up by the base handle.

Make sure tables and chairs are clean and free of dust, crumbs, food and trash. Check that the floors are clean.

Look under table tops to make sure there is no gum.

Check condiments on table to make sure they are clean, full and pour freely.

Table tops should be set up correctly and look the same.

Be sure to initial the checklist sheets to insure that all tasks get done. Although, some of the tasks on the checklist can be done during your shift, NEVER let them interfere with or be a priority to guest service.

Check your appearance. We want our servers to look clean and professional before approaching tables.

Know Your Menu

Before you are ready to serve our guests, you should have your menu memorized. You can ask the manager for a copy to take home, if it will help you. Knowing the menu will give you more confidence when you walk up to a table.

You need to know the bar menu as well. It's important for you to be able to make suggestions to guests. The more you learn about the beer and wine offered, the more you will be able to suggest a pairing to go with the guests' meal(s).

Sometimes guests can be allergic to different foods, so you need to know the ingredients used in preparing each menu item.

Know the portion size and quantity of each menu item. Sometimes guests don't have a big appetite. Also familiarize yourself with the cooking time and preparation methods.

Be aware of the different sauces used as well as what is served with the meal (side dishes, fries, etc.).

Check with the kitchen at the beginning of your shift to see if they are out of any menu items, if there are any substitutions or if there are any specials. You need to be able to suggest alternatives to guests if there are any items that are not available on the menu. Don't forget to check with the bar to see if there is anything unavailable or if stocks are low on any items.

If there are specials, practice reciting them until you feel comfortable enough to recite it to a guest.

Answering the Phone

When you answer the phone, the person on the other end needs to hear a smile in your voice. They need to feel like you're glad they called.

Try to answer the phone within 2 rings. The standard phone greeting is: "Thank you for calling _____. How may I help you?"

If you are asked a question that you can't answer, politely ask them to hold while you go find out what it is they want to know.

Make sure that you know what the hours of operation are.

ALWAYS have a pen, an order pad and a menu handy in case someone needs to place a take-out order.

Service Sequence

Host/Hostess will assign tables to each server and will check to see if any reservations have been made.

Host/Hostess will meet guests within 30 seconds of entrance and will greet them using the proper time of day, Good (morning, afternoon or evening), welcome to _____ (always cheerful and with a smile)! If they are frequent diners, be sure to use their names, whenever possible. This can be done by saying "I've noticed that you are a frequent guest. My name is _____. What's yours?" Then say "Well, we're glad you came back, Mr. /Mrs. _____. Pass this along to their server, so that they can call the guest(s) by name, as well. It's important that our guests feel welcome!

Host/Hostess will inquire as to how many people are in the party and obtain the correct number of menus and silverware rolls.

Host/Hostess will seat guests, pulling out the chair for the eldest female in the group. Menus will be presented from the left while thanking them for joining us and making light conversation. Let them know who their server will be. Be sure to ask if they are there for any special reason or celebrating anything. Their server will need to be informed, if they are.

Server will approach table and greet guests within 1 minute of their being seated. Be sure to smile and make eye contact. Then greet them with, "Welcome to _____. My name is _____, and I will be your server this (morning, afternoon or evening)! If they are frequent diners, be sure to use their names.

Alcohol Service

You must be 18 years of age in order to serve alcohol.

ALL servers are required to be state certified.

Know the state regulations as well as the restaurants policies for serving alcohol and be sure to abide by them.

Be sure to announce "Last Call" to guests at least 30 minutes before closing time.

Taking and Delivering Orders

ALWAYS smile every time you approach a table. First, offer the guests a drink by asking, "Can I get you something from the bar?" If they want something that is not from the bar, they will let you know. NEVER say "Would you like something to drink?" Ask if their orders will be together or separate, if there is more than one couple or they are part of a group. This will save you from having to split their tickets later. Take ladies orders first, starting with the eldest, going clockwise around the table. If there are children, take their order(s) next.

Then, offer them an appetizer by asking "Would you like an appetizer while you are waiting for your meal? Our _____ (choose any appetizer) is a favorite of most of our guests." Give a description of the appetizer in such a way that it creates a craving.

Up-sell whenever you can. The more menu items you sell to a guest, the higher their check will be and, possibly, the bigger your tip will be. Make sure to speak clearly and offer affirmations when they are ordering (i.e. excellent choice, that's one of my favorites, etc.). Just be friendly.

Repeat the order to confirm it before you leave the table. This gives guests the opportunity to change their mind and ensures that you have heard the order correctly. Write down table number, number of guests and your initials at the top of your order. Keep the written order in your pad until the end of your shift. This is to back you up in case a mistake is made.

Input order into the POS system (see next chapter) so the kitchen can get started on the appetizer(s). Then get the drinks ready.

When putting ice into glasses, be sure to use the scoop. NEVER scoop up ice with the glass or use your hands. Return ice scoop to a receptacle. DO NOT leave the scoop in the ice bin.

Then take the drinks back to the table. Drinks should be served within 3-5 minutes after they have been ordered. NEVER touch the rim of the glass or put your hand over the top of the glass when serving. Hold glasses by the stem or base. If you are serving iced tea, take an iced tea spoon with a napkin beneath it. Put the napkin with the iced tea spoon on the table to the right of the guest and place the glass above the spoon.

Server will then take the meal order, beginning with the eldest lady. Notify customers of any unavailable items and offer alternatives. If someone is ordering an appetizer instead of an entrée, be sure to ask them if they want it as an appetizer or as a meal. Be sure to ask all pertinent questions such as what kind of salad dressing they would like or how they would like their steak cooked? Again, repeat back the order to confirm selections, prep styles and sides before leaving the table.

Now is the time to announce the dessert selections for them to think about. Pick a dessert and give a detailed description that will make them want to save room for it.

Be sure to pick up the menus. If you notice that a menu is messy after you pick it up, give it to the hostess to clean.

Enter the order into the POS system. Appetizers should be ready and delivered within 10 minutes of order. Hold plates by the rim with fingers away from the food. Be sure to warn guests if the plates are hot. Serve guests from their left, eldest ladies first.

Check back in 2 minutes to make sure everything is satisfactory and to see if any drinks need refilling. ALWAYS ask about refills when you see that a glass is half full. When refilling drinks, pick up the glass from the base and hold it away from the table if pouring from a pitcher.

Check back in 5-10 minutes to see if they are done with their appetizers. If so, clear all of the appetizer dishes off of the table taking dishes from their right. Crumb the table off by brushing crumbs into your hand or a plate with a napkin or clean cloth.

When picking up your order from the kitchen, check to make sure it is your order and that it is correct. There are a lot of orders coming out of the kitchen and you don't want to take the wrong one to your table. You are the last one to see this order before it gets to the guest(s), so make sure that it is correct and what the guest ordered. This is also an opportunity for you to make sure the presentation is what we want our guests to receive (i.e. not sloppy looking, sauce wiped off of the edge of the plates, etc.).

Entrees should be served within 15-20 minutes of initial order. ALWAYS carry out plates on trays. Hold plates by the rim with fingers away from the food. Be sure to warn guests if the plates are hot. Serve the eldest lady first. Remember to serve guests from their left.

Ask guests if you can get them anything else and check to see if they need refills. Guests should never have to ask for refills. If guests ask for extra napkins, give them one extra napkin per person and only give out straws if guests ask for them. Don't automatically put them on the table.

Check back within 2 minutes after food has been served to make sure that everything has been cooked properly and tastes good. This is our chance to fix anything that the guest may be unhappy with.

ALWAYS stand where you are visible to your tables in case a guest is trying to flag you down. Try to anticipate the guest's needs and never give them the opportunity to have to ask for something.

Make sure all guests are served in a timely manner and assist other servers as needed. Remember you are part of a team.

Check back every 6 minutes to make sure everything is satisfactory and to ask if you can get them anything else. Be sure to remove any empty dishes, taking them from the right of the guest. If you sense that guests don't want to be interrupted, do a visual check. Items to look for when doing a visual check are; plates pushed aside, guests not eating, drinks needing to be refilled, lap napkins on the table or plates, etc.

When guests are nearing the end of their meal, see if they would like dessert by asking if they would like to try the dessert that you previously described or like to see a dessert menu. Remember to up-sell. Also ask if they would like coffee, tea or milk with their dessert.

Clear entrée dishes from the table and crumb the table before bringing the desserts out. Dessert and after-dinner drinks should be served within 5 minutes of ordering and brought out on a tray. All desserts should be standing upright and served with the face or point facing the guest. Ask if you can get them anything else and tell them to enjoy their dessert. Remember: NEVER leave the dining room empty-handed. There is always something you can take off of a table, even if it is not your table.

Entering orders

Find an unoccupied POS system and enter your order. You should have already entered the appetizer, if the guest ordered one. If that's the case, then you will need to pull up that same order to add to.

POS training will be done by a manager.

Take your time and make sure the order is entered correctly. Be sure to use notes if there are special instructions for the kitchen. Double check the order before sending it to the kitchen. Put yourself in the cooks place to determine if they will understand what you are trying to get across. This will help to insure that you get your orders to the guests correctly.

If you need help entering an order, don't hesitate to ask a team member or manager.

Handling Complaints

Because we want our guests to have a good dining experience every time they dine with us, we rely on our servers to use good judgment in order to make this happen. When a guest is not having a good experience, it becomes an opportunity for us to turn the situation around by the way we handle problems or complaints.

If a guest has a complaint, the first thing to do is to really listen to the complaint. Use direct eye contact to show that you are interested in what they are saying. Ask questions regarding the problem and repeat the problem to make sure that you understand fully what the problem is. Apologize. Make sure that they feel you are sincere. You can't apologize enough.

NEVER place blame or explain why the situation occurred. Guests usually don't care. They just know they are not having the experience that they expected. Even if there is a good reason for what happened, it's still going to sound like an excuse to them. Simply apologize and show empathy for their bad experience. For example, a guest complains they had to wait over 20 minutes for a table. It's not anyone's fault, but we can apologize and let them know we understand.

Immediately, notify the manager of the problem so that a quick solution can be found.

If an item needs to be returned to the kitchen, notify the manager and show him/her the item, as well as the chef. Have the item re-cooked, if applicable. Returned food should be given top priority in the kitchen. All re-cooked items should be delivered personally by the manager.

Only the manager has authorization to comp a meal. If the meal is to be comped, it should be done before presenting the check to the guest.

Follow up to make sure the problem was resolved to the guest's satisfaction.

Thank them for bringing the problem to our attention, because it gives us the opportunity to improve our service.

It is our responsibility to make sure that each guest leaves our restaurant with the intention to make a return visit.

Check Presentation

Before presenting the check, make sure to verify that all items have been rung up. When the guest is finished with their meal, ask them how everything was and if they would like anything else. If not, lay the check tray on the table to the left of the person that you think may be responsible for paying. Thank them and tell them you will take it for them whenever they are ready.

Make sure you know what forms of payment are accepted. If credit cards are accepted, know which ones.

Return to table within 3 minutes to pick up the payment. Take payment to cashier. If you have a credit card, return the card to the guest with two receipts. One is the restaurants copy and one is the customers copy. Highlight the area on the restaurants copy where the guest is to sign to ensure that it is seen. **When you give** them the receipts, tell them that you need to get the signed copy back. It is VERY important for you to get the signed copy back and it is YOUR responsibility. If you do not get a signature on the credit card receipt, you will be responsible for paying that check total.

If they give you cash, return their change as soon as possible. Try to give them enough change to make it easy for them to leave a tip. Return to the table to pick up the trays <u>before</u> the customer leaves so that you can thank them again, invite them back and insure that they have signed the credit card receipt.

Reset Tables

Clear the table(s) off and clean the tables well, moving condiments to be able to clean under them. Wipe off chairs. Make sure there is no food or crumbs on tables or chairs. Check your condiments to see if any of them need to be wiped off or refilled.

Leaving Early

During times when the restaurant is slow, you may be asked to leave early. When this occurs, you will need to complete the serving of your tables and your shift duties before leaving. Talk with your teammates to work out which duties you will be responsible for and need to complete before you leave, but keep your customers your first priority. Taking care of guests is far more important than completing your shift duties in a timely manner.

If you have an emergency and can't complete your shift, you first need to talk to the manager. Then you will find a teammate to take over your remaining tables. You and the server taking over for you will go to each of your tables so that you can explain to the guests that you will be leaving, but _____ will be taking over for you and will continue to give the same good service that you have been giving.

Tips

Tips are never solicited or expected. Remember tips are based on good service. The better your service, the better your tips will be.

Tip-outs will be done by a manager at the end of your shift. Don't forget about tip sharing! Be sure to share your tips with any teammates who may have helped you during your shift, such as other servers, busters, bartenders, etc.). When the entire team works together, the customer receives better service.

Discrepancies with tips should be discussed quietly and in private with the manager.

Make sure you record your tips where indicated when you clock out. If you do not do this on your own, management will be forced to do it for you, and possibly at a higher percentage rate.

General Safety

Wipe up spills immediately. If you need to mop the floor, be sure to put out the "Wet Floor" sign.

Try to clean as you go.

ALWAYS announce yourself when carrying food or drinks (i.e. "Behind you!" OR "Hot plates!").

NEVER run in the restaurant!

DO NOT leave the restaurant alone at night. Find someone to walk you to your car or walk out with someone else who is leaving at the same time.

ALWAYS cooperate in the event of a robbery.

Know what the procedures are for a fire or other emergency.

Closing Side Work

All closing side work is to be done before clocking out. Make sure work area is ready for the next shift by putting yourself in the place of your teammate(s) who will be coming in next. Do for them what you would want them to do for you.

You are not to leave until a manager has checked your work and has authorized you to leave.

Let's all work together to make this a great place to work

and a place that guests will want to return to

for a wonderful dining experience!!!